Why Do Horses Have Manes?

With lots of love to Vincent, Cherokee, Dillon, Sera, Rory, Fleet, Big Mack, Ari, Tipton, Tessie, Toodles, Puzzle, Marmalade, Jet, Blue and _____ (add your favorite horse name here) — LM

Why Do Horses Have Manes?

By Elizabeth MacLeod

Kids Can Press

Kids Can Press acknowledges the financial support of the Government of Ontario, through the Ontario Media Development Corporation's Ontario Book Initiative; the Ontario Arts Council; the Canada Council for the Arts; and the Government of Canada, through the BPIDP, for our publishing activity.

Published in Canada by
Kids Can Press Ltd.
29 Birch Avenue
Toronto, ON M4V 1E2

Published in the U.S. by
Kids Can Press Ltd.
2250 Military Road
Tonawanda, NY 14150

www.kidscanpress.com

Edited by Karen Li
Designed by Marie Bartholomew
Printed and bound in China

Photo Credits

Every reasonable effort has been made to trace ownership of, and give accurate credit to, copyrighted material. Information that would enable the publisher to correct any discrepancies in future editions would be appreciated.

Abbreviations: t = top; b = bottom; m = middle; l = left; r = right

p. 1: Mladen Mitrinovic/Shutterstock; pp. 2, 12, 43(b): Alexia Khruscheva/ Shutterstock; pp. 5, 18, 26(b), 39, 42, 45: Eric Isselée/Shutterstock; p. 6: Jeanne Hatch/Shutterstock; p. 9: Jeff Banke/Shutterstock; pp. 13(b), 34(b), 40(b), 43(t), 49(b), 53, 54(t), 61, 63(t): Stephanie Ellul/Fantasporadic; p. 15: courtesy NASA; pp. 22(t), 24(t), 26(t), 36, 48: Marie Bartholomew; p. 23: Jessi Zamboni, CheyAut Ranch, New River, Arizona; p. 24(b): Daniel Naccarato; p. 25: Michael Steden/Shutterstock; p. 27: (t) Susan Randfield, (b) Winthrop Brookhouse/ Shutterstock; p. 29: Pavel Pustina/Shutterstock; pp. 32, 38, 52, 60(b): Abramova Kseniya/Shutterstock; p. 33: (t) CarlaVanWagoner/Shutterstock, (t-l) Christian Scaraglino/Shutterstock, (t-r) Justyna Furmanczyk/Shutterstock, (b-l, b-m) Claudia Steininger/Shutterstock; p. 34(t), 59: Eline Spek/Shutterstock; p. 35: Laila Kazakevica/Shutterstock; p. 37: Guilu/Shutterstock; p. 41: Ellen Beijers/ Shutterstock; p. 44: (t) Justyna Furmanczyk/Shutterstock, (b) Karen Powers; p. 46: (t) Jose Lopez Montero/Shutterstock, (b) emmanuelle bonzami/Shutterstock; p. 51: Karen Givens/Shutterstock; p. 55(t): Podfoto/Shutterstock; p.57: Arkadiy Yarmolenko/Shutterstock; p. 58: GSK/Shutterstock; p. 60(t): Zuzule/Shutterstock; p. 63(b): Vyacheslav Osokin/Shutterstock.

All other photos © 2009 Jupiterimages Corporation.

Many thanks to consultant Dr. Brian Hancey, Main Street Animal Hospital, Cambridge, Ontario; and to Ronnie Roumeliotis and Sharon Simon.

This book is smyth sewn casebound.

CM 09 0 9 8 7 6 5 4 3 2 1

Library and Archives Canada Cataloguing in Publication

MacLeod, Elizabeth
    Why do horses have manes? / Elizabeth MacLeod.

ISBN 978-1-55453-312-1

1. Horses — Miscellanea — Juvenile literature. I. Title.

SF302.M33 2009   j636.1   C2008-903257-8

Kids Can Press is a CORUS™ Entertainment company

Contents

Chapter 1

When Horses Flew

For millions of years, horses have trotted over the earth's surface. It's hard to believe, but they were once about the size of cats, and they slunk around in swamps. Gradually, they grew and evolved to look like the animals we know today.

For a time people hunted horses for meat, but it wasn't long before mares and stallions were instead domesticated for their muscle. The speed, strength and beauty of horses inspired people to tell stories about both real and imaginary horses and horselike creatures. Humans and horses have a long history together of racing, jumping, working — or just hanging out.

〜 〜 〜 〜 〜 〜 〜

Why do horses let people ride them?

As long as 15 000 years ago, people in Europe hunted wild horses for food. Then they began herding them like sheep. These people were nomads, which means they moved around a lot. They soon discovered that horses could help by carrying the heavier bundles and pulling large loads on sleds. Perhaps someone scrambled up on the back of a horse to adjust a pack. Or maybe a person climbed onto a horse to see farther. Soon people discovered the advantages of horseback riding. Some horses were too wild to be ridden, but others had learned to trust their owners and were comfortable with carrying them on their backs.

Famous horse lovers

Actor Viggo Mortensen, a star of the Lord of the Rings movie series, bought two of the horses he rode in the films. Kate Bosworth grew up riding horses and so did Hilary Duff, who also helped an organization that protects wild horses in the United States.

How smart are horses?

Horses are very smart. Just ask anyone whose horse has figured out how to get out of her stall! Horses have good-sized brains, but a lot of their brainpower is taken up just trying to keep four feet in motion, especially when quickly going over rough ground.

Horses easily learn through repetition, either by themselves or by watching other horses or humans. As long as they're trained consistently, they can learn to recognize commands and body language. Horses also have an uncanny ability to find their way home, sometimes even over unfamiliar territory. Pretty smart!

U U U U U U U U U U U U

What did the first horse look like?

Picture a little creature about the size of a cat. It has thin legs, a short neck and a blotchy coat that blends into its surroundings. Its front feet have four toes each, and its back feet have three toes each. That was the first horse, and it lived about 60 million years ago.

Then the environment around this creature changed from marshy swamps to open plains. So the little animal, called *Hyracotherium* or *Eohippus*, began to evolve, too. It no longer needed multitoed feet to keep from sinking in the soft earth, so it developed a single hoof. Its legs grew longer to help it run quickly from enemies. Then its neck had to become longer so it could reach down to eat grass. The animal kept changing until it looked like the horse we know today.

Today, the horse's relatives include zebras, wild asses, donkeys and mules.

Measuring up

Long ago, people buying horses didn't carry tape measures. If a buyer wanted to know a horse's height, he used a measuring unit he always had with him: the width of his hand. The unit was named a "hand" and is 10 cm (4 in.).

A horse's height is measured from the bottom of its feet to the top of its shoulders, or withers. That's about how high off the ground a rider will end up sitting. What if the height doesn't work out to an exact number of hands? If a horse is 17 hands and 2 in. (5 cm) tall, he's 17.2 hands high or 17.2 hh.

How fast can a horse run?

Top speed for a racehorse is about 69 km/h (43 mph). That means the horse is one of the ten fastest mammals in the world — and that's while carrying a jockey on its back!

How high can a horse jump? How far?

In 1949, Huaso set the high-jump record when he leaped over a jump 2.47 m (8 ft., $1^1/_4$ in.) high. Imagine a horse sailing over the head of a pro basketball player! The long-jump record belongs to the horse Something. In 1975, he jumped a width of 8.4 m (27 $^1/_2$ ft.) — that's longer than a minibus.

∪

Horse talk

Quit horsing around and see how many horse expressions you know! (Answers are below.)

1. If you're told to hold your horses, should you (a) speed up or (b) slow down?

2. One of your friends is a horse of a different color. Is she (a) like all your other friends or (b) not?

3. When you've put the cart before the horse, have you (a) done things in the wrong order or (b) arranged everything perfectly?

4. If you put on the feedbag, do you (a) grab a snack or (b) get dressed up?

5. Someone says, "Hoof it!" Should you start (a) kickboxing or (b) walking?

Answers: 1. b, 2. b, 3. a, 4. a, 5. b

What's a Trojan horse?

For ten years, an army of ancient Greeks had laid siege to the city of Troy. Then one morning, the people of Troy awoke to find the Greeks gone and a huge wooden horse outside their gates. Deciding it was a peace offering, the Trojans dragged the horse inside and began celebrating their victory.

That night, while the Trojans slept, Greek soldiers crept out of the hollow horse. They opened the city gates for the rest of the army hiding outside and finally conquered Troy. Today, a Trojan horse also means a computer program that looks harmless but is very destructive.

What's the oldest horse ever?

The horse Old Billy lived up to his name. He was born in 1760 and lived to be 62. That's about 150 in human years (see page 45). Most horses can live for 20 to 30 years if they're well cared for, or about 16 years in the wild.

Uffington White Horse

High on a hill in south-central England, a huge white horse sprawls across the grass. The Uffington White Horse is 110 m (361 ft.) long, and experts think it has been there for about 3000 years. Ancient people created the figure by carving trenches 1.5 to 3 m (5 to 10 ft.) wide, then filling them with bright white chalk.

What does the horse mean? No one knows for sure. It may be a symbol of a long-ago tribe. Or maybe it was an ad saying "Horses for Sale!"

Work horses

Horses were likely first tamed about 6500 years ago by people of Central Asia. The pack animals were soon ridden into war, then later used in farming. By the 1700s and 1800s, horses became vital for pulling plows and other farm machinery. They also dragged barges along canals. They towed streetcars and delivery wagons. Pit ponies lugged carts of coal deep in mines.

In North America, horses hauled immigrants in covered wagons westward across Canada and the United States. The legendary Pony Express depended on horses to help deliver the mail.

Horses still work hard. They carry cowboys and perform in circuses, parades and other events. They take part in sports, such as horse racing, polo and rodeos. Police horses control crowds and help with search and rescue. Therapy horses work with physically disabled people, and some miniature horses even work as guide animals for the visually impaired!

What's a hippogriff?

This mythical animal is a cross between a griffin (a beast like an eagle) and a horse (*hippos* is the Greek word for horse). Harry Potter befriended one.

The legend of the centaur — half man, half horse — may have started when people began riding horses and nonriders didn't understand what they were seeing. Other legendary horses include Pegasus, the flying horse, who helped Greek gods and heroes. When he died, he was made into a constellation. The unicorn is a magical horse with a single horn on its forehead. Today, people think narwhals or rhinoceroses inspired tales of this creature.

Why are horseshoes lucky?

One story tells how the devil once noticed a horse galloping through town. Its horseshoes sparked on the cobblestones as it ran. The devil thought this looked great and commanded the local blacksmith to make him horseshoes.

But when the blacksmith nailed a horseshoe onto the devil's hoof, the devil roared in agony. That's because the devil's hooves are sensitive, not like a horse's hooves. The blacksmith removed the shoe, but whenever the devil sees a horseshoe, he still remembers the awful pain and steers clear!

What's the Year of the Horse?

If you know someone born in 1978, 1990 or 2002, then according to the Chinese zodiac your friend's a Horse. That means he's strong, enthusiastic and confident, but he can also be selfish, gullible and quick-tempered. Nelly Furtado, Nelson Mandela and Adam Sandler are all Horses.

Famous horse match

Can you pair the description of each celebrity horse with its name? (Answers are below.)

Famous Horse

1. Seabiscuit
2. Black Beauty
3. Snowfire
4. Spirit
5. Big Ben
6. Comet
7. Secretariat

Description

a) "Stallion of the Cimarron"

b) Helps Supergirl fight crime

c) Large show-jumping horse

d) One of the greatest racehorses ever

e) Eragon's great white horse

f) Dark hero of a book with the same name

g) This racehorse's name is a type of cracker

Answers: 1.g, 2.f, 3.e, 4.a, 5.c, 6.b, 7.d

Chapter 2

Paints, Percherons and Palominos

From the huge Percheron to the tiny miniature horse, horses come in a wide range of heights, weights and body types. These characteristics combine in different types of horses, or breeds, and are then passed on to their offspring.

Horse breeders raise breeds with specific looks or skills that fill particular roles. The Hanoverian excels at show jumping, while the Friesian has been bred to pull carriages. Reared in the extreme conditions of the desert, the Akhal-Teke can withstand scorching days and freezing nights.

Keep reading to find out about the many beautiful and fascinating horse breeds.

How many breeds of horses are there?

There are about 150 breeds of horses, as well as about 80 breeds of ponies. Here are the ten most popular horse breeds in North America:

Quarter horse
the quarter-mile champion

Paint
sports a blotchy or "painted" coat

Thoroughbred
a fast, athletic racehorse

Tennessee Walker
easygoing and known for its unique walking style

Standardbred
strong legs make it a great harness racer

Appaloosa
a spotted American horse

Arabian
a beautiful and very ancient breed

Anglo-Arab
combines Arabian and Thoroughbred traits

Morgan
a smart show horse

Saddlebred
a high-stepping horse that's popular in parades

∪ ∪ ∪ ∪ ∪ ∪ ∪ ∪ ∪ ∪ ∪

What's the difference between a horse and a pony?

Horses stand at least 14.2 hands — that's 147 cm (58 in.) — at the withers (shoulders), and ponies are generally shorter. Also, ponies usually have thicker manes and tails than horses. Horses tend to have longer legs, thinner necks and longer heads.

What's a miniature horse?

These little creatures stand less than 9.2 hands or 96.5 cm (38 in.) at their withers. So they're the size of a pony, but they tend to have the slimmer build of a horse. Miniature horses are friendly and were once the pampered pets of royalty.

∪

Which breed is which?

Match the horse breed below with the correct characteristic. If you'd like to see what these breeds look like, have an adult help you check the Web for photos. (Answers are below.)

Breed

1. Rocky Mountain horse
2. Bashkir Curly
3. Norwegian Fjord
4. Icelandic horse

5. Falabella
6. Australian stock horse

Characteristic

a) Smallest breed in the world

b) Uses a unique trot to get around Iceland's rough ground

c) Bred to work in the outback "Down Under"

d) Has a thick, curly winter coat

e) Viking horse seen in ancient carvings in Norway

f) Can tolerate freezing mountain weather

Answers: 1. f, 2. d, 3. e, 4. b, 5. a, 6. c

Is a palomino a breed?

A palomino's golden coat and shining white mane and tail are a striking combo. But palominos are a color type, not a breed. This coloring can be found in many horse and pony breeds. The coat color is described as "the gold of a newly minted coin."

No one knows for sure where the name palomino comes from. It may have originated with a Spanish nobleman, Juan de Palomino, who had one of these beautiful horses. Palomino is also the name of a golden grape from Spain. But in that country, these horses are often called "Isabella" after the Spanish queen who encouraged people to breed these horses.

Scotland's tough little pony

The Shetland pony is probably the world's best-known "little horse." For its size, it's also one of the strongest.

This pony comes from the cold, bleak Shetland Islands, just northeast of Scotland. A meager diet of rough grass and small plants stunted the Shetland's growth and made it tough.

Today's ponies still grow a double coat in the winter, and their tails and manes are thick. Extra large nasal cavities warm the chilly air before it hits the little animal's lungs. The Shetland walks with a lift to its knees that it learned from moving over the islands' rocky ground.

∪ ∪ ∪ ∪ ∪ ∪ ∪ ∪

How did the quarter horse get its name?

Many people claim the quarter horse is the most popular horse in the world. Cowboys love this horse because of its agility, speed and instinct for working cattle. Farmers love it because it is hardworking, whether hauling lumber or being ridden.

People began racing the compact, muscular horse, and it couldn't be beaten over a quarter-mile (0.4 km) stretch. One reason is that its massive hindquarters, or quarters, give it power for an explosive racing start. So this horse gets its name from both its speed and its shape.

Are there still wild horses?

Przewalski's horse, also known as the Mongolian wild horse, is the only true wild horse still alive. It has never been domesticated, which means it has never been trained to live and work with people.

Around the world are groups of horses whose ancestors were once domesticated but later escaped or were abandoned. Today their descendants live in the wild. These horses are called feral and tend to be small and tough.

Mustangs are feral horses that roam wild lands in the United States and Canada. In Australia these horses are known as brumbies.

The Sable Island pony lives on Sable Island, off the coast of Nova Scotia. To the south, off Maryland and Virginia, feral ponies live on Assateague Island. The Assateague and Chincoteague ponies were made famous in the book *Misty of Chincoteague*.

The Exmoor pony still roams the moors of southwest England. Namibia has Namib desert horses, while Spain and Portugal are home to the Sorraia horse.

Which horse can pull the heaviest load?

The strongest horse breed is the Shire. It's descended from England's Great Horse, the steed that carried heavily armored knights into battle during medieval times. Despite its warlike ancestors, this horse is known today as the "Gentle Giant" because of its size and docile personality.

In 1924, a Shire known as Vulcan pulled an amazing 47 tonnes (51¾ tons). That's more than the weight of eight elephants! No wonder the strength of modern engines is described as "horsepower"!

∪ ∪ ∪ ∪ ∪
When is a horse not a horse?

When it's a water
horse, a sea horse
— or a hippo! Hippopotamus means "river
horse," but hippos are actually more closely
related to pigs than to horses. Sea horses have
horselike heads, but they are actually
fish. And if you've seen the movie
The Water Horse or read the book,
then you know that a water horse looks
less like a horse and more like the
Loch Ness Monster!

What's the biggest horse ever? The smallest?

The tallest horse ever was Sampson at just over
21.2 hands high — that's 2.2 m (7 ft., 2 in.).
Sampson was also the heaviest horse, weighing
1.5 tonnes (3300 lb.). No wonder he was
renamed Mammoth!
    Thumbelina is the world's smallest horse.
This dwarf miniature horse stands 4.1 hands
high, or 43 cm (17 in.), and weighs just
26 kg (57 lb.).

∪

Make a horse bookmark

Find a photo of your favorite horse breed in a magazine or on the Web, or draw your own. Choose a full-body side view, as in the photo below, so that you can clearly see all four of the horse's legs. Paste the photo on thin cardboard. Then cut out the horse. If its legs are very thin, you might want to leave a border around them.

To use your horse as a bookmark, place one front leg and one back leg on the front side of the page you're marking. Slip the other two legs behind the page.

Face it!

Horses can have many kinds of face markings. You can probably guess what chin spots and white face — sometimes called bald face — look like.

Here are the names of some other face markings:

A **strip** or **stripe** is a narrow white line down the middle of a horse's face.

A **blaze** is like a strip but wider.

A **snip** is a small white mark between a horse's nostrils.

A **star** is a small white mark that's positioned on the horse's forehead.

Do some horses really have feathers?

Yes, but a horse's "feather" is the long, silky hair that grows just above some horses' hooves. It's beautiful, and it protects the leg. Feather directs rain or water to run off the leg, rather than pool and cause sores.

Heavy horses especially known for feather include the Ardennais, the Clydesdale and the Shire.

Spot the horse

The Appaloosa, the famous American spotted horse, was bred by the Nez Percé tribe of the Pacific Northwest. The Palouse River runs through the area, so White settlers called the animal the "Palouse horse." Eventually, the name became Appaloosa.

This eye-catching horse is also strong and good-tempered, with great endurance. The Appaloosa's mane and tail are short and sparse so they won't catch on thorny shrubs.

〜 〜 〜 〜 〜 〜 〜 〜 〜 〜 〜 〜

What's so special about Arabian horses?

Some people say that the Arabian is the most beautiful of all horse breeds, and there's no question that it's the oldest. Because of this, there are many stories about the origins of this courageous but gentle horse.

The Bedouin people, who live in the deserts of Asia and Africa, say that God created the Arabian horse from the four winds. The winds gave the horse spirit, speed, strength and intelligence. Another tale says the Arabian came out of a tornado and was first known as "Drinker of the Wind."

An Arabian's bone structure is different from every other breed's. The Arabian's wide chest; short, strong back; sloped shoulders and high tail give it a floating way of moving.

Chapter 3

The Mane Tale

Horses are prey animals. That means they don't hunt other animals for food but instead are hunted. Horses have survived because they have keen senses that allow them to pay close attention to their surroundings. Even today, pampered pets still have the instinct to shy at a rustling plastic bag or a loud noise that's a long way away. With their long legs and powerful muscles, horses are built to run from danger. Their bodies have many other adaptations to keep them safe from predators.

Why are horses so good at running?

Horses have no sharp claws or teeth to defend themselves against enemies. Their best defense is to run away. So their bodies are built to make them fast runners.

A horse's long legs quickly cover lots of ground. Their bones and muscles are built for forward and back strides. Like you, and some other animals, horses also have special muscles that let them store energy between gallops. By running on tiptoe (see page 39), horses increase the length of their stride. And their feet are built to absorb the shock of each landing.

Horses have one more speed secret: running pumps their lungs to make breathing easier.

♘ ♘ ♘ ♘ ♘ ♘

Can horses really sleep standing up?

"Hooks," called stay apparatus, in a horse's back kneecaps can lock the horse's knees. This allows the animal to sleep on its feet. Sleeping upright allows horses to make a quick escape if threatened.

Why do horses walk on tiptoes?

Walking on tiptoes makes a horse's stride longer and helps the horse run faster. See that joint halfway down a horse's front legs? It looks like a knee, but it's actually similar to your wrist. On the hind legs, the joints that point back are its hocks, which are like your ankles.

A horse's hoof is made of the same material as your nails. Walking on tiptoes would crack your nails, but hooves are a much stronger version of this material.

♘

Why do horses wear shoes?

Horses' hooves evolved for life on dry plains. But when horses were domesticated, they had to walk on rough roads or through wet fields. So horseshoes were created to prevent hooves from tearing, becoming sore or wearing unevenly. Horseshoes also give horses good grip.

The first iron horseshoes were created almost 2000 years ago. They were tied to the horse's feet and called hipposandals! Eventually, the shoes were nailed to the horse's hooves. But hooves are made of the same substance as your fingernails so attaching shoes doesn't hurt. Some people feel that with proper diet and care, horses don't need to wear shoes at all.

Play a game of horseshoes

All you need to play are two sticks about
25 cm (10 in.) long, a stretch of clear ground and
two horseshoes per player. Cut out your own from
foam or heavy cardboard. Make them at least as
big as your hand.

  Poke your sticks into the ground about
9 m (30 ft.) apart, or closer while you're learning
the game. Each player stands at one stick and throws
his two shoes toward the other stick. Shoes that land
15 cm (6 in.) or less from the stick count for one
point, and "ringers" — shoes that circle the stick
— count for three. The game is
over when someone scores
40 points or you've each
thrown 40 shoes.

Horse sense

A horse can quickly sense nearby threats. It doesn't have great eyesight but, like most prey animals, its eyes are on either side of its head, so it can see almost right around itself. A horse can't see anything directly behind it or very close to the center of its face or right under its neck.

A horse's hearing is much keener than its vision. Horses can detect and identify sounds. They can hear both lower and higher sounds than humans.

Ever notice how a horse reacts when a fly lands on it? That's because a horse's entire body is as sensitive as your fingertips. The horse can feel a fly on a single hair. As well, the long hairs around its muzzle and eyes help it feel how far it is from an object.

42

U U U U

Baby horses

When a baby horse,
or foal, is born, it
may weigh anywhere
from 20 kg (44 lb.)
if it's a Shetland pony, to 70 kg (150 lb.) if
it's a Shire horse. Most foals are born at night,
perhaps because the mothers (dams) don't like
to be watched while they give birth.

Whether the newborn is a filly (female) or
colt (male), its legs may already be as much as
90 per cent of the length they'll be when full
grown. Within a few hours of being born, the
foal can walk. It took you about a year to do
that! But for foals, it's important to be able to
run from danger.

U

⌣ ⌣ ⌣ ⌣ ⌣ ⌣ ⌣ ⌣

Nice to 'ear from you!

A horse's ears are incredibly mobile. It has ten muscles attached to each ear — you have only six. So if the horse wants to hear something behind it, it can turn its ears almost right around.

A horse can also use its ears to signal how it's feeling. If the ears are pricked forward, the horse is interested in its environment. If one ear faces forward and the other faces back, he's uncertain and so trying to pick up clues from all around. And when a horse's ears are pinned back against its head, look out! She's angry.

Can you tell a horse's age from its teeth?

Yes, if you know how a horse's teeth change as it grows older. For instance, the incisors (the biting teeth at the front of the mouth) slope forward as the horse ages. The molars (the grinding teeth at the back) get worn down from chewing. As well, all the teeth turn yellow.

⌣

How old are you in horse years?

Use this chart to calculate your age in
horse years. How old are the people
in your family?

Human Age	Horse Age
1 year	1 month
2 years	2 months
3 years	4 months
4 years	6 months
5 years	8 months
6 years	10 months
7 years	1 year
8 years	14 months
9 years	16 months
10 years	1½ years
11 years	20 months
12 years	22 months
13 years	2 years
16 years	2¾ years
18 years	3 years
20 years	3½ years
22 years	4 years

‿ ‿ ‿ ‿ ‿

Water guzzler

Horses will drink
an average of 45 L
(180 c.) of water
daily. That's about as
much as 23 large milk cartons, or approximately
23 times as much as an adult human should
drink every day. Like you, a horse needs water
to keep food moving through its system and to
stay healthy.

Where is a horse's frog?

Some of the parts of a horse
have very strange names.
Here are just a few of them:

barrel: a horse's trunk or torso

cannon: a thick bone located in
the lower half of the leg

chestnut: horny growths on the
inside of all four of a horse's legs

dock: the solid part of a horse's
tail, not the hairy portion

frog: a shock-absorbing pad on the
bottom of a horse's hoof

stifle: like your knee; on a hind leg

Flea-bitten and bloody shouldered

Horses' coats come in an amazing range of colors, from white to black. Some of the names of those colors are very strange. For instance, a "flea-bitten" horse has a white or gray coat with freckles of red hair. A "bloody shouldered" horse is very flea-bitten, usually on the shoulder.

The Bedouins prized bloody-shouldered Arabian horses. They told a tale of a warrior who rode his brave Arabian mare into battle. The warrior was badly wounded and fell across the mare's shoulder. Balancing her master on her back, the mare carried him home. When they arrived, her master was dead and her shoulder was stained red from his blood.

The mare soon gave birth to a colt. Her master's family gasped when they saw him — he had the same red shoulder markings as his mother! The Bedouins felt God had rewarded the mare's courage with this symbol. From then on, a bloody shoulder was considered valuable.

Hungry as a horse

Horses like to eat a little food all the time — this way they're never slowed by a full stomach while escaping from an enemy. As well, a horse's digestive system works best when it's partially full. The system is also built to get the most out of plant fiber, which is why horses can survive when food is scarce.

One thing a horse can't do is vomit. As in your stomach, a one-way valve at the top of a horse's stomach keeps food from going back up the throat. But a horse's valve is stronger than yours, so nothing moves up past it.

The nose knows

A horse depends on its nose to sniff out danger, find the best food and locate other horses. So in dusty winds, horses can close their large nostrils to protect them.

Why do horses have manes and tails?

A horse's mane protects the animal's neck from bites — by bugs, other horses or predators. Along with the forelock (the hair between a horse's ears), the mane may also help direct rain off the horse.

A horse swishes its tail to brush off flies. It also uses its tail to show how it's feeling. When the tail hangs straight down the back of its legs, the horse is anxious. It's excited if its tail is stiff and pointed up. And when the tail hangs light and loose, you've got a calm horse.

ᘮ ᘮ ᘮ ᘮ ᘮ ᘮ ᘮ ᘮ ᘮ ᘮ ᘮ ᘮ ᘮ ᘮ

Chapter 4

Straight from the Horse's Mouth

If someone tells you something's "straight from the horse's mouth," it means the information comes from a reliable source, and you can trust it.

Horses may not talk, but they definitely have many ways to communicate. Learn them, and you'll become what cowboys call "handy" with horses.

The most popular names for horses are fairly short — Charlie, Rosie, Jack and Molly — perhaps because trainers know horses can be taught to recognize short words and their meanings. But to a horse, the tone — how the words are spoken — is also very important.

ᘮ

Neigh! Snort! Squeal!

Horse noises may sound similar, but listen closely. When a horse blows gently through its nose, it's relaxed or curious. If a horse snorts, it's trying to figure out if there's danger nearby.

No one knows for sure what a neigh or whinny means, but it likely keeps horses in touch with each other. A nicker or soft neigh can mean many things: Stallions nicker at mares to say, "You're cute." A mother horse nickers to her foal to call it closer. One horse may just greet another with a nicker.

Horses squeal or roar when they're preparing to fight.

Who's who in a herd?

For a prey animal such as a horse, living in a herd makes sense. While the other horses graze, one watches for danger. For the same reason, horses sleep better in a group because some animals stay awake and alert.

The leader of a herd is often an older mare. She gives clear directions to her group about where to go and when, and she has the trust of the other herd members. Horses are comfortable when they have a strong leader to follow. They sometimes fight to find their place in the herd, but they know they have to stick together to survive.

Why do horses nuzzle and groom?

Nuzzling and grooming are ways horses communicate. Touching like this feels good and says "We're friends" or "We're in the same herd." Grooming a horse's shoulders also calms the animal and even lowers its heart rate. That's why people gently scratch their horses there.

Aren't I handsome?

When a horse feels good or pleased with itself, it lets you know by strutting around proudly. Here's how to read other horse moves and postures:

Head and eyelids drooping, standing on three feet: the horse is totally relaxed

Foot stamping: the horse feels angry

Head and neck stretched out with ears forward: the horse is curious

Hindquarters swinging: the horse is getting ready to kick

♘ ♘ ♘ ♘ ♘

Strange friends

Horses are herd
animals, so when
there aren't other
horses around, they make friends with other
animals, such as cattle, sheep and pigs.

Goats are supposed to calm nervous horses,
so they're sometimes brought into the stables of
high-strung racehorses. Some people think the
expression "get your goat," meaning to irritate,
comes from the trick of stealing a racehorse's
goat-friend so it will race badly.

Horses also make
friends with smaller
animals, such as cats,
dogs and even rabbits.
Jack, a horse who lives
near Montreal, Quebec,
has a Flemish Giant
rabbit for a pal. Another
horse got so used to
having rabbits in its
stable that it refused to
eat unless its long-eared
friends were nearby!

♘
55

Horse heroes

Ever since soldiers first saddled up, horses have bravely carried their masters into battle. During World War One, horses also delivered messages and carried supplies. These amazing animals knew to neigh when they heard enemy planes but stay silent when their own fighter planes roared overhead.

Horses have been heroes in peacetime, too. On a cold winter night in 1978, the Morgan/quarter horse Indian Red drew people's attention to an elderly woman who had collapsed in a snowy ditch in Ontario. He likely saved her life. More recently, Max, a quarter horse, and Lady, a Shetland pony, protected their owner and her two daughters from a vicious dog.

In 1998, a young Percheron named Phoebe slipped down a Kentucky riverbank into the swirling waters below. Rosie, the filly's mother, jumped in and placed her big body on Phoebe's downstream side. That kept Phoebe from being swept away. Rosie neighed for help and stayed with her filly until both horses were rescued.

Horse detectives

Horses have keen senses of smell, hearing and touch. But some people think horses can pick up on much more. There are many stories of a horse trotting along peacefully — then suddenly refusing to move forward. Later, the rider will discover an accident or murder has taken place at exactly that spot.

It's known that horses can sense fear, anger and other emotions in people. As well, they really dislike the smell of blood. Perhaps a horse's super senses make it react so strongly. Some people believe that horses are even sensitive enough to be aware of ghosts and spirits.

What's a horse whisperer?

About 200 years ago, Daniel Sullivan, a horse trainer, became famous for his work gentling horses that had become vicious because of abuse or an accident. Sullivan wouldn't reveal his methods, so some people tried to catch a glimpse of him at work.

The spies saw Sullivan stand face to face with a horse and assumed he was talking quietly in a special way the animal understood. The horse quickly became well behaved, and Sullivan gained the title of "horse whisperer."

Today a horse whisperer is a trainer who uses tactics based on how horses interact with each other, rather than using force.

∪ ∪ ∪ ∪ ∪ ∪ ∪ ∪ ∪ ∪ ∪ ∪

How do Lipizzaner horses do their amazing tricks?

The gleaming white horse leaps high into the air and kicks out his back legs. Another stands up on his hind legs and hops with grace and power. They can only be the famous Lipizzaner horses.

These horses are born bay (reddish brown) or black, and they whiten as they age. Lipizzaners begin practicing when they're about four, and it takes six years to fully train them. These strong, compact horses have naturally good balance, train well and are very smart. Their tricks are called the "airs above the ground" because they involve the Lipizzaners being completely or partially airborne.

♘ ♘ ♘ ♘ ♘ ♘
Goin' for a gallop

The walk is the slowest of a horse's speeds, or gaits, at about 6.4 km/h (4 mph). The left hind leg moves, then the left front, the right hind and finally the right front, making four beats.

Twice as fast as the walk, the trot is the main way a horse travels quickly. This two-beat gait involves moving diagonal pairs of legs in unison.

The next faster gait is the canter, which is a three-beat stride. A rear foot and a diagonal front land together, while the other two feet strike separately.

At about 48 km/h (30 mph), the gallop is the fastest gait. Listen and you'll hear four beats.

Walk, trot, canter and gallop are the basic terms for English riding. In western riding, the terms are walk, jog, lope and gallop.

Why do horses roll on the ground?

Rolling on the ground feels great to a horse. It rubs off sweat, scratches any itches, gives his feet and legs a rest and lets him stretch out the muscles of his spine, neck and more. Horses in a herd usually roll in the same spot, and they especially like a clean, sandy place.

Why aren't police horses afraid of loud noises?

Police horses go through tough training. They must overcome their natural instincts to run from bangs and flashes. First, trainers carefully select horses for police work. The animals must be brave, relaxed and smart. The training starts slowly, perhaps with someone clapping in the horse's face. Eventually, the horse learns to stay calm during gun blasts, fire and blaring music.

Most police love the horses. They say one officer on horseback is like twelve on the ground. Sitting high above traffic or a crowd makes it easier for police to spot trouble.

Horses up close

If you see a horse at a show or fair and want to pat it, show your horse smarts and follow these tips:

- Only approach a horse whose owner says it's okay to come closer.

- Don't approach a horse from behind — it might think you're trying to sneak up on it, and the horse may kick you.

- Keep your arms down at your sides or the horse could see you as big and a danger.

- Don't spread out your fingers — a horse might see them as claws and be frightened.

- Speak softly as you get close so the horse is aware of you.

U U U U U U

How can you tell if a horse likes you?

If a horse runs toward you and whinnies, it's easy to tell he likes you. Other clues are that he's calm and doesn't try to kick or bite. Ask the owner if you can rub the horse between the ears and you'll definitely make a friend!

What's the best way to give a horse a treat?

Only give a horse a treat after checking with its owner. Giving a horse too many treats may make it pushy, or "muggy," as horse people say. Place the treat on the palm of your hand with your fingers flat and together. Otherwise your fingers may look like delicious carrots. Ouch!

U

Horse laughs

A big, noisy laugh is sometimes known as a horse laugh. See if these jokes make you and your friends laugh that loud!

Q: What can horses have that no other animal can?
A: Baby horses!

Q: What's the hardest part about learning to ride a horse?
A: The ground!

Q: What does it mean if you find a horseshoe?
A: Some poor horse is walking around in his socks!

Q: A man rode into town on Tuesday, stayed three days and rode out on Tuesday. How is this possible?
A: His horse was named Tuesday!

Q: Why couldn't the pony sing?
A: Because he was a little hoarse (horse)!